UNFORGOTTEN AUGUST

Sunnie Antonio Marcar Jr

UNFORGOTTEN AUGUST

Published in Ghana in 2021 by
Firstline Publisher
Tabora Junction, Accra
P.O. Box KS 314,
Adum, Kumasi
firstlinepublisher@gmail.com

© Sunnie Antonio Marcar, Jr. 2021

Request for the permission of copyrights and additional copies of this book can be made through:

E-mail: mccaflakes@gmail.com

Phone: (+231) 777 867 648 / 888 405 988

Printed by: QualiType Ltd., Accra

Cover Design: Sylvester Edem Baah

ISBN: 978-9988-3-2035-5

To
Mr. Sunnie Boima Marcar Sr.
&
Mrs. Antoinette Blamo Marcar,
my beloved parents

TABLE OF CONTENTS

FOREWORD

For approximately three years, it has been my pleasure knowing Sunnie Antonio Marcar Jr in a friendship that has escalated to co-workmanship and partnership in developing writers and poets of Liberia. I have watched him grow in his writing career and seen him add value to scripting the thoughts of his mind.

I always had a love to read actual Liberian stories, and I have been blessed to share many of them with my family and friends as well. But when Sunnie told me about his book, 'Unforgotten August', I was intrigued. There is no story that is not worth being told.

Every day I see people doing great things in the world. What do they have in common? The courage to go after their dreams and make a positive impact. Sunnie's book shows how that message can support you in running your life and business based on courage, love, and kindness instead of fear, although life has its way of trying to direct one's path.

The tragic story of the girl plays a real scenario in my head especially being in Liberia and knowing how difficult things are. Having such a bad experience caused by the epidemic is not anyone's wish, but recovery from the devastation is a blessing.

"Unforgotten August" will give you a deeper insight into the actual stories of how people are afflicted with epidemics and how many lives are stagnated due to the outbreak of illnesses and diseases. This book will definitely stimulate your desire to help them overcome rapidly.

Put yourself in the victim's shoes and prepare for a voyage of both sadness and happiness.

Cheers,

William P. Anderson
Author: "Black Man with Metaphors"
President, Liberian Poet Society

ACKNOWLEDGEMENTS

The publication of "Unforgotten August" would not have been fruitful without the blessings and strength of God Almighty and the narrations of Patience Stewart, Siatta Stewart, Joe Y. Gono, Korto Gono, and Malah Popo; to them, flowers are given.

Thanks to the following individuals who contributed by proofreading and editing: Lekpele M. Nyamalon, William P. Anderson, Peter S. Dewellie, Momodu Gray, D' Siafa Draper, Emmett K-Max Paye and Anita C. Cooper. Also, to the folks: Grandma Musu Conneh, Ma. Siatta Pabai Gray and Sedia M. Dukuly who narrated their traditional birth ceremony; I say thank you.

Lastly, appreciation goes to the Liberian Poet Society and Dominion Technologies Incorporated for providing structural and publishing guidelines.

INTRODUCTION

Minds have sworn never to divorce the memories of the year 2014; for the matrimony that unified them filled their cups with sorrows and made them tossed against a glass of calamity. As the orchestra of mourning played, those who danced could no longer dance so they stood in awe; those who sang could no longer sing, so they hummed, and those who feasted on bowls of grief were filled so much that they threw out instead.

"Unforgotten August" is a true story of a Liberian girl who became an orphan after she lost seven members of her family to the deadly Ebola plague that rubbed shoulders with Liberia in 2014 – her mother, her father, one of her brothers along with his wife and daughter who were both pregnant, her aunt, and her cousin.

It further narrates how over 5,000 heads bowed to the deadliest and longest Ebola epidemic in history in the year 2014.

Until now, Patience still suffers the darkness that engulfed her eyes and the horrible nightmare to which she unwillingly said '*Yes I Do*'. The melanin of her beautiful black skin conceals the unseen scars left behind by the wreck of the year 2014.

The inscriptions on these pages narrate how she slipped through the claws of death and ran into the arms of life. Now, she sniffs on an aura of survival; a strong black woman, wanting to cloth in a nightgown of courage and prepare for the nights ahead.

CHAPTER ONE

Patience's Birth

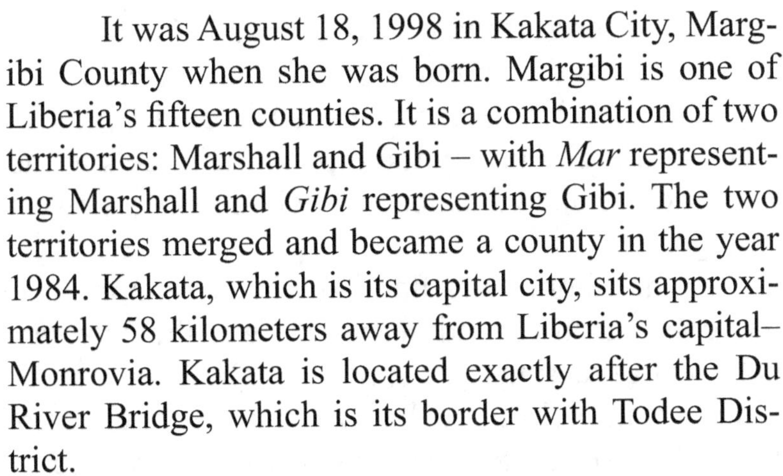

It was August 18, 1998 in Kakata City, Margibi County when she was born. Margibi is one of Liberia's fifteen counties. It is a combination of two territories: Marshall and Gibi – with *Mar* representing Marshall and *Gibi* representing Gibi. The two territories merged and became a county in the year 1984. Kakata, which is its capital city, sits approximately 58 kilometers away from Liberia's capital–Monrovia. Kakata is located exactly after the Du River Bridge, which is its border with Todee District.

As a tropical region and an agricultural belt, Kakata experiences heavy rains. Sometimes, the angry wind and August rain beat the roofs of homes so hard that it sounds like a roaring lion. At times, heavy storms remove the roofs of buildings, exposing their floors to flooding.

Amidst the heavy downpour of rains and inimical weather, the birth of a beautiful black girl was unstoppable. On August 18, 1998, Ma. Fatu – as was commonly called – held tight the pillars of pain and gave birth to a beautiful black queen.

As would happen in most communities in Liberia, when a child is born, the neighbors run through the community singing and dancing. For the joy of the day, it is usually the pot tops and empty gallons that suffer, as they are beaten in anxiety for melodies. When the child was born, so it was. The neighbors paraded the community singing the old traditional song: *Bobo Na Bo, Bobo Na Bo.*

On that day, lightning danced in the cold blue sky and thunder declared the birth of a beautiful black child. The family too dipped their heels in the unfriendly mud and danced to welcome their newest stranger.

Their home was flooded with neighbors who had come from far and near to shower the newborn baby with greetings and gifts. Her Dad, being a religious man, held the belief that children were gifts from God, so, he too was anxious in acceptance of the newborn child; she too was a 'Gift from God'.

Most Liberian traditions have it that when a child is born, the child remains indoor for six days and on the seventh day, the child is brought out for a naming ceremony. The naming ceremony for children varies among the 16 tribes of Liberia. As for the

Vai tribe to which Mr. Stewart belonged, the child is kept indoors for six days, and brought out on the seventh day. On the seventh day, an eponym comes outside with the child in their hands or places the child on the floor in the doorway at the entrance of the house.

Thereafter, the eponym names the child after her/him by whispering their name in the child's ears with a few words:

"From today, your name is ... You will be like me. No one will overcome you. You will grow and be stronger than your friends. You will succeed in whatever you put your hands in."

After the child is blessed, the eponym blows spit in the child's face and turns the child over to the parents, who in turn bless the child.

Traditionally, the person who names the child also gives a lappa to the mother and instructs her as follows:

"This is my lappa. Tie me on your back with it and take good care of me."

At the naming ceremony, cassava leaf soup, the favorite food of the Vai is prepared. Rice dust is also pounded and mixed with honey and placed on a plate along with kola nuts beside it. Those who attend the ceremony also eat the kola nuts and pounded rice.

According to Liberian tradition, a 'kola' is usually money, kola nut, or mostly domestic animals used to welcome strangers.

Although Mr. Stewart was of the Vai tribe, he was a staunch Christian whose religious belief superseded his traditional belief. Therefore, on a Sunday after the child was born, she was prayed for, and named *Roseline Patience Stewart*.

CHAPTER TWO

Patience Moves to Monrovia

Patience, as was affectionately called, opened her eyes beneath the roof of discipline. She was born in Gbandi Community behind the Calvary Baptist Church, opposite the Messiah Day Care School in Kakata. Her parents lived in a big maroon and black house. Their yard, plastered with sandy soil has gravels with grass growing in-between. At the left front of their house, a large leafy tree makes a canopy of shade during the day. At the front right is a Monkey Apple tree whose fruits the kids feed on. Beautiful domestic flowers also kiss the sidewalls of their home.

When Patience turned two years old, she was taken by her aunt to reside with in a community called Shara Community, located in Duport Road. While growing up in the Duport Road community, Patience spent most of her vacations in Kakata with her parents. There, she mingled with an extended family of fourteen members. She was last among five sisters and two brothers. With her parents, were some of her cousins, foster brothers, and other relatives.

Growing in an extended family was fun for Patience. She was enveloped in a company that kept her animated. Patience was not lonesome because she had around her a crowd of relatives and friends. Like a sprout of rose, she was tied up in the warmth of roses; yet, pricked by thorns of responsibilities. The older folks were a *star in the east,* and in them, she found a shelter when the storm blew.

Patience's father, Mr. F. Molly Stewart, was a Preacher man at the Zion Assemblies of God Church in Jambo Village, Kakata. He raised his family in the doctrine of Jesus Christ. Mornings and evenings, he would gather his family at their home altar in devotion to God. During devotion, the family sat at the feet of their father as he fed their minds with the scriptures and watered their thoughts with testimonies.

"Train up a child in the way he should go; and when he is old, he will not depart from it," [Proverbs 22:6] is the most familiar scriptural quote Patience remembers falling from her Dad's mouth.

Though her Dad was a Preacher man, her ambition was not to become a preacher woman. However, her steps were ordered by him so that she would not become less than a human.

On Sunday mornings when Patience was in Kakata, she would complete her home chores and prepare for church service. Having their church within their community give them the advantage to skip a few lanes across the streets to worship. At times, they would ride a commercial motorcycle for at least twenty Liberian dollars per person. Most Sundays, Patience would walk to church with the *Preacher man*, her brothers, sisters, and cousins.

As a common proverb says: *'Behind every successful man, is a woman'*; and Ma. Fatu was that strong woman behind the *Preacher man*. She coordinated domestic activities and served as a Sunday school teacher at the church. Between both parents, Patience was closer to her mother than her father.

Unlike the 60s and 70s when boys were sent to schools and girls were held in high esteem of domestic chores or sent to the *'Bush School'*; the 90s onward unfolded a dramatic U-turn. Considerable attention is now given to the education of the girl child and Patience was of no exception. She attended the Action Faith Institute; a private school located in Duport Road where she lived. For uniform, she wore a navy-blue jumper, white t-shirt decorated with three red stripes at the neck, hand, and pocket. A blue pair of socks and a black pair of shoes comforted the soles of her feet.

When the echoes of the morning birds caressed the earth, Patience woke up early morning to prepare herself for school. She wore an ambitious smile as she marched to school along with some of her friends from her neighborhood. As a child, she yearned for education and cherished the comfort of her friends in her neighborhood and her teachers at school.

Though Patience was fed with the warmth of a family, she needed an external soulmate to confide in. At school, she found Gbehme a companion. Happenings of the day were the conversations that kept them alive while they both travelled to school. Patience and Gbehme's friendship was knotted in age and empathy. Moreover, Gbehme was good at mathematics which made her a great asset to Patience. Patience describes Gbehme as a tall, dark-skinned girl with long hair.

Within her neighborhood, Sianneh was a friend whom Patience associated with since they lived closer together. She describes Sianneh as a short, light-skinned girl with small eyes. On weekends, Patience and her friends roamed about in their neighborhood with the other children playing hopscotch, lappa, knock-foot, tic-tac-to, hide-and-seek, and other familiar Liberian games.

On Sunday afternoons, Patience visited some of the neighbors to plait her hair, and afterward, would return home to complete her home chores.

As a routine, every Sunday evening, Patience had to prepare her uniform and dip her head in her books to prepare for the new school week. These were the excitements that nourished her soul and cheered up her growth.

When days lifted the banners over months and years, age was one great inheritance that those many years left. Patience was gradually sprouting into an adolescent girl. She had turned 15 years old – an age she knew herself better. Her half-brother Ezekiel attended the University of Liberia and was a sophomore student studying Education at the William V.S. Tubman College of Education at the University of Liberia.

Christopher, her cousin from her father's succession had already graduated from high school and was preparing for college. One of her cousins – Jackson from mother's lineage also resided with the Stewarts in Kakata. Jackson and Gray who were cousins to Patience, both attended the Lango Lippaye High School – the only public high school in Kakata City.

Most parents who could not afford the sky-rocketed cost at private schools, found government schools *a port in a storm*. Not that learning at these institutions is not effective, most public schools in Liberia lack infrastructural and technological facilities, which made private schools the best alternative. In terms of instructions, the majority of teachers who teach at public schools in Liberia *whirled on wheels* to teach at private schools. Though public schools are seen as *a port in a storm*, they have produced some of the brightest and prominent leaders in society.

Patience's eldest sister Famatta, who is only a high school graduate, resides in Kakata. Siatta who is the next sibling to Famatta, is a graduate of the University of Liberia where she majored in Management. Her third sister Abigail is a high school graduate and Margret, Patience older sister lived in Monrovia and was at the edge of her secondary school that year.

As an adolescent, Patience recalled a blissful and disciplined family – a family where children were served their rights accompanied by domestic responsibilities; a family whose sail was directed by a religious captain headed towards a shore of contentment. Her joy and comfort sprouted out of the limbs of her family, and as a child, she enjoyed the showers of love poured upon her head by her parents. Patience and her family lived in a nation where access to pipe-borne water, electricity, and the internet was found mostly in urban communities.

As for Kakata, a peri-urban community, the main source of domestic water was either the pumps, wells, or nearby creeks.

Whenever Patience visited her parents in Kakata, her home chores were to fetch water in small barrels for cooking and to wash dishes. Every morning and evening, Patience would go to the community well to fill her bucket with water.

She would place the bucket on her head and haul water into her home. She also had to sweep, clean her parents' room and the house. On most weekends, she had to mob and dust up their home too.

Though the Stewarts never had much, life for them was travelling on the *path of constellations;* for their little was much because God was in it.

CHAPTER THREE

Ebola Outbreak in Liberia

A year had elapsed and it was March 2014. Sweet hip-co melodies from Tycoon-J and other Liberian musicians still complemented the New Year. The glowing morning sun happily lighted the small city of Kakata. Every evening, Mr. Stewart fed his ears with the news while he sat on his veranda studying the Bible and preparing his sermons.

One evening, Mr. Stewart's excitement grew into fear when the news headlines carried the story of the outbreak of the Ebola virus in Liberia.

On the 21st of March 2014, the Ministry of Health in Guinea reported the outbreak of the Ebola Virus Disease in West Africa – an illness characterized by high fever, severe diarrhea, vomiting, and high fatality rate.

It is believed that Emile Ouamouno a two-year-old boy who died in December 2013 in the village of Meliandou, Guinea, was the index case of the soon-to-be largest and longest Ebola epidemic in history. After little Emile *travelled in pine coat*, his mother, sister, and grandmother then became ill with similar symptoms and also *gave up their ghosts*. People infected by those initial cases spread the disease to other villages, and then to Liberia – a country bordering Guinea – at the end of March 2014. By this time, March was about to welcome few weeks of sunshine before the rainy season.

In late March 2014, the fear of the virus dressed the headlines of every news outlet in Liberia. The state radio Liberia Broadcasting Corporation (ELBC 99.9 FM) reported that the Ebola virus was detected in Lofa County in a patient who had returned from Guinea where the outbreak began.

Subsequently, *the beast* took up heels and travelled into the nation deep. Many who were suspected to have been bitten by the beast now sought assistance within the national healthcare system; leading to various outbreaks among health workers throughout Liberia.

Initially, when the rising tides bowed to the land of Liberia with news of the outbreak, it was denied and backlashed with many different misconceptions. One myth had it that it was the Liberian government's strategy to attract donors' funds while another had it that it was a strategy of discouraging the consumption of sweet bush meat – especially monkey meat which many Liberians love.

Several Liberians denied the outbreak of the virus; forgetting a common Liberian proverb: "*Where there is smoke, there is fire*" and surprisingly, there was fire. Indeed there was fire; a wildfire that would soon burn down the fabrics of many West African nations and set them to ashes; a wildfire that would sooner or later smoke the dwellings of every creature, both humans and animals alike.

On 7th April 2014, five cases were confirmed by the Liberian government: four in Lofa, one in Monrovia, and all patients bowed to the dust. Towards the end of April, 34 cases were carved on the record of the epidemic and six souls answered to the call of death.

Like a shaken glass of coke, the situation arose and later stabilized, with no new cases reported in Liberia at the end of April through May.

After a few sunsets and dawns, like a phoenix, the epidemic reincarnated. By 17th June 2014, seven patients died from the disease; a nurse along with other members of her household.

On July 2, 2014, the head surgeon at the Redemption Hospital shook the hands of death after being treated of Ebola at the John F. Kennedy Medical Center in Monrovia. His death shocked the nation with fear and the doors of the Redemption Hospital were bolted. Patients were now being transferred or referred to other facilities in Monrovia.

The storm started to rise again and, by July 21, 2014, four nurses at Phebe Hospital in Bong County contracted the disease and died.

Towards the end of July 2014, tens of people had succumbed to the call of death – most of whom were health workers. Many health workers started falling prey to the epidemic because most initial cases were thought to be malaria; thus, leading to health workers being carriers and transmitters of the virus.

The flames of the fire grew brighter and its heat spread wider from villages to towns, and cities, and to the 15 counties of Liberia. The walls of clinics and hospitals became swollen from patients' billows so much that health workers who feared being stung by the beast retrieved from the battlefield; yet, others laid down their lives for their country.

The roots of the epidemic were now deepening into the soil of every county; including Margibi, in which Patience lived. The news of an epidemic that was going to be the deadliest and longest in World's history was now confirmed.

Doctors and nurses began to fall prey to the claws of the epidemic. The country's organs and systems were driven on a path of thorns and dust. The curtains of calamity were about to open wide to many homes; turning them into kingdoms of mourning.

The 'Preacher man' knew how deadly the Ebola virus was – owing to the history of how it destroyed the lives of thousands of Congolese who lived along the bank of the Ebola river (where the virus got its name) in Zaire in the year 1976. He always told his family and congregation to pray for the nation; emphasizing that it was only God who could deliver them.

Despite how perilous the Ebola virus was; many Liberians did not initially take heed. Perhaps, it may have been that many were not knowledgeable or the catastrophic claws of the epidemic had not scratched the beautiful face of their virgin nation.

Sadly, people continued business as usual. Until cases of Ebola began to increase in the country, people were still laissez-faire about the outbreak; yet, others were conscious. Those who were conscious began to sound a caveat of the dark clouds that would soon blanket every sector of the nation; a dark cloud that would cause troubling winds to blow the dust of calamity over West Africa.

The situation of the epidemic intensified with more people getting sick and many deaths occurring. *Seeing is believing*, they say, and those who wished to see now saw bodies abandoned in homes and along the sidewalks of the streets of Monrovia.

Bodies were left for stray dogs and rats to sniff

on, bodies were left to decorate the shoulders of the streets of Monrovia. Cultural norms were forbidden. When those who wished to see now saw this, they believed and took heed but it was a little too late.

The cold dew of the morning watered the already wet land with songs of mourning. A day laid ahead when only the dead were going to bury the dead and ashes were going to be the only memorial for fallen loved ones. Indeed, *where there is smoke, there is fire* and the flames were hot and blazing. One awareness message said: *"Do not eat bush meat"* and another said: *"Do not touch sick or dead people"*.

From the terrible news headlines to the screams of sorrows that were heard from dawn to dusk; every ear longed for the gospel – a day when the storms were going to be over and Liberia was going to be Ebola-free; a day when people would once again hug and shake hands in the old traditional way.

CHAPTER FOUR

Patience Visits Kakata

Since 1847, July 26 has been celebrated as Independence Day in Liberia. It is an illustrious holiday characterized by feasting, visitation, and fun. But as the sails of Liberia's Independence Day drew closer, so was the shadow of the Ebola epidemic. 'Twenty-six', as is usually referred to by Liberians, is a day when the pockets and nooks of every street get decorated with strange faces; a day when the ears of Liberia listen to her favorite melodies and her eyes see her favorite dances.

Now that the storm of death and mourning were blowing over her, "what good was it to be free? What cause was there to celebrate?" Instead of listening to her favorite independence song, Liberia listened to her famous funeral song – *It is well with my soul.*

At that time, Patience had gone to visit her parents in Kakata to spend the Twenty-six; a day that kindled the most memorable holiday for her – one that stands between twilight and midnight. It was the day she had *the last supper* with her parents.
She recalled her mother buying food and drinks to prepare for the holiday. On that day, she woke up early to assist her mother and elder sisters prepare food.

Patience was just about to turn a year older and her 16th birthday was knocking at her door. By then, she knew how to cook – she had been a friend to the kitchen for a decade. For the holiday, there was plenty of food to prepare; not only for their family, but also to share with their neighbors and visitors who came around.

For Patience, it was fun being in the kitchen; she had a taste of every bit and piece and drowned herself in the crust of delicious soups.

Prior to holidays, people have plans about where to go and what to do. Patience, her siblings and her friends also had plans despite the epidemic. Part of their plans were going to visit friends, relatives, and planning what they were going to eat and drink.

Finally, when the day was ripe and bright, Patience sat at the table and had '*the last supper*' with her parents and other members of the family. Subsequently, she along with her friends headed on a journey of fun – to visit relatives and friends and get magnetized by the side attraction of the streets.

On that day, Patience recalled wearing blue jeans and a black t-shirt. In spite of the epidemic, the kids had fun visiting places, relatives and friends. At last when the sun was falling into the belly of the ocean, the heap of darkness took Patience beneath the shadow of her roof and she closed her eyes in memory of the day.

On the day that followed, the death of Dr. Samuel Brisbane – one of Liberia's top doctors – was completely *out of the blue*. Soon, a doctor from Uganda was also killed by the virus. In the days that followed, two U.S. healthcare workers; one a doctor (Dr. Kent Brantly) and the other a nurse were also infested with the virus. Both of them were missionaries, and on August 2, 2014, they were medically evacuated to the US for treatment.

CHAPTER FIVE

Patience's Parents Death

In the beginning, all was good for little Patience – food to eat, a home to sleep and a family that loved. At dawn, she was awakened by the melodies of the morning birds that set the pace for a happy day. At midday when she went out to play, the overhead sun drove her shadow beneath her feet and poured sweat down her skin. At dawn, she had to fetch water for her home, shower and prepare for dream's land.

Indeed, everything was good, good until dawn forced a bitter capsule down the throat of a sweet land of liberty; a sweet land that was now turning bitter. For its cities, it was only the cries and the bombshell of the deceased that dominated the news headlines. 'Ebola' was a trending news on state radio ELBC 99.9 and community radio stations in Kakata including Radio Kakata and Radio Joy Africa.

An eye-catching headline on one newspaper read: *"Ebola hits Liberia the hardest"*

Prior to the outbreak of Ebola, the crows from roosters and the chirpings of morning birds were the signs of a new day in Liberia. But not as usual, in 2014, sounds of cries and sirens were welcoming trumpets to new days – days that cuddled a nation with fear and sorrow; days that broke darkness instead of lights.

Seconds had turned hours into days; then came August when the storms of pain blew heavier through droplets of rains. August, unforgotten August – the same August when Patience was born; an August when it rains *'cats and dogs'* in Liberia. Lightning dresses up the skies and thunderstorms threaten the caps of homes. For decades, people in the hinterlands of Liberia observed a seven-day consecutive rainfall in August.

As usual, they were now preparing for the seven days August rain; gathering food in their barns and wood to keep them warm.

In Kakata, it was always wet and cold. Once upon a time, Patience drew her curtains to watch the children of her community play under the rain. Sometimes, she sat on their porch and watched them sing *'Rain-Rain go up, potter-potter come down'*. On other occasions, she stood by the window and watched blue jays sing from a tree next to her window; but most often, she would bench in the kitchen around the coal pot warming her body. The year 2014 was different. That year, she benched on sorrows and awaited the misfortune of the coming days. August in Liberia is a preparatory month for the reopening of schools in September. But in that year – 2014, August was a month when Hades gate opened to receive thousands of grudging souls. In the corridors of the classroom marched a dreadful beast that sealed the doors of schools and vowed to teach Liberians their lessons. Before the feet of learners, the gates of schools bolted out.

The path that led to the Cross for worshipers was dark and narrow and the roads to markets were quiet as graveyards.

By August, the epidemic had widely spread and hundreds of heads had nodded 'yes' to the call of death. The guts of graves were filled so much that bodies were cremated. Though individuals and institutions had begun to create intense awareness, it may have been a little too late, as many people had ignorantly contracted the virus by touching sick people, treating them at homes, and seeking treatment at high-risked facilities.

As for Patience, great fear embraced her innocent soul and she felt sadness walking into her life. She heard the whisper of tragedy through the sound of the rain that danced on the rooftop. Her mother had already fallen severely sick in early August. With rumors that engulfed the city of Kakata, many feared to seek treatment at health facilities.

Consequently, Patience's mother was treated at home by two elderly women who were relatives of hers – Ma. Malah and Ma. Korto.

Though she was treated at home, in the days that followed, Ma. Fatu showed no sign of recovery. The more drugs were administered, the worse her condition became. As the clock ticked, nights passed away but the hope of the Stewart's remained.

It was Sunday morning, August 10, 2014. Ma. Malah who is a sister to Ma. Fatu was indoor caring for her nauseating sister. She refused to abandon her nor leave her at the mercy of her illness, not even for a day. Though their family tree may have bent, she refused to allow it to break. Ma. Fatu was so ill that her sister literally cleansed and fed her. With severe weakness, high fever and headache, no one knew it was Ebola.

On that fateful morning of August 10, 2014, Ma. Malah recalled:

"I prepared food for my sister and heated water for her bath. She was not eating solid foods so I used to feed her with the water from the rice crust. I can remember that Sunday morning…. I prepared hot water for her and took her to the bathroom for Patience to bath her. After bathing her, I fed her and she came outside to sit in the kitchen.

"That Sunday, her husband was preparing for church service. He came and said to her 'Fatu, I'm going to church, please give me an offering.'

"I had some money for my sister Fatu and she asked me for a portion of it. I gave her a thousand Liberian dollars which she gave to her husband and he went to church.

"It didn't take any time when Fatu said to me 'Ma. Malah, I want to eat oh'.

"You are eating plenty today oh," I said to my sister.

'If I don't eat, you complain, if I eat plenty you will still complain. What do you want me to do now?' My sister asked and we laughed about it.

"That morning, I fed my sister again and after eating, she went inside to lie down. Suddenly, she called, 'Hellen... Hellen...'. Her granddaughter Hellen went inside to see why she was calling. Soon, I followed to see what was going on and when I arrived, my sister Fatu said to me 'I can't see you. I can't see you again'.

"My heart leaped and I became afraid. Not knowing what to do, I called some of the children to help and bring her outside. We brought her outside in the sitting room and placed her on a mat. She was sitting on my feet with her back resting on my knees.

"I stood behind her to support her. This time, she grunted 'I can't see you again'. She started to speak from her throat and I could barely hear her.

"It was Sunday morning, I remembered. My sister was sitting on my feet. That morning, my sister jerked heavily and opened her mouth wide, as if she was laughing. After a few minutes, she stopped moving and I called 'Fatu! Fatu! Her body was heavy and stiff. She looked in one direction with her eyes open and not blinking."

At this, Ma. Malah's forehead creased. Her eyes became sour, and the beat of her heart sounded louder than the African sambal. She drew her lower lip between her teeth. Her brows kissed and held closer together. Her eyes spewed hot silver droplets onto her cheeks. In panic, she screamed 'Fatu!'

"When I called; 'Fatu! Fatu!' and she didn't answer, I knew she was dead."

Ma. Fatu's eyes became stable as a rock and a rosy glow on her cheeks signaled that the warmth of life had departed. Her face stood as peaceful as the east and her body laid quietly on the mat. It was about 10:00 that early morning when Ma. Fatu died.

Choruses of cries echoed towards Heaven's gate, and like a rushing wind, the rest of the family members ran into the sitting room only to find their mother laying dead. Like tributaries of rivers, tears oozed down the eyes of her children, and grandchildren. They all dashed themselves on the floor and on the gravels that plastered their yard.

That which Patience greatly feared, had now fallen upon her head – a weight too heavy to bear.

The neighbors too made a fence around them and folded their hands gazing amazingly.

Mr. Stewart was yet to come from church and upon his arrival, a cloud of crowd and songs of mourning beckoned that death had embraced his family. He was astonished by the news that greeted him.

He dashed through the yard and rushed into their porch only to find his wife laying dead.

Standing over the corpse of his wife, he looked upward and asked the heavens: "God, where are you?"

He remembered the words of the Holy Scriptures: *'Never will I leave you, never will I forsake you' [Hebrews 13:5]*.

But on the contrary, it seemed to him that this didn't hold water because not even a seed from his prayer fell on fertile grounds nor a line from his request returned answered from the Heavens. Now that his soulmate was dead, he feared that there was nothing to hope for. He requested the immediate burial of his wife but a few members of the family, and his church opted for a religious burial sacrament.

In no time, Ezekiel, the son of Ma. Fatu, his cousin Christopher and few other members of the church collected the remains of their mother with their bare hands and drove her corpse to the Margret Funeral Parlor – a nearby funeral home along the

C.H. Rennie Hospital road in Kakata. Upon arrival at the Funeral Parlor, the burial team was notified and arrived to intervene.

In consultation with the family, a compensation of US$ 75.00 was paid to the burial team and subsequently, the burial was performed and the corpse of Patience's mother was taken to the dust. Clouds had turned dark for the Stewarts and the shooting stars did not grant the family their wishes.

In mid-August, cases of the epidemic began to erupt randomly. Death crept through the heavy rains and embraced hundreds of souls, leaving the lives of thousands at stake. The walls of homes were being stained with blood and the latches of eyes were watered with cups of tears that mourning served. The minute hand on the wall clock was now measuring the number of deaths as it ticked.

Music was now sorrow for the soul instead of food and the friendly rains in which children played stirred up muds of mass graves. Reality had fallen on those who believed and those who disbelieved.

August 18 of that year stamped Patience's 16th birthday. On that day, she had nothing for which to celebrate. It was exactly six days after her mother – whom she loved best – departed the earth. The memories afresh still danced in the corridor of her mind and synchronized drills of her father's sickness. Liberia was now dressed in black, mourning for the hundreds that had fallen and the thousands that were yet to fall.

The week that followed brought severe headache and cold upon Mr. Stewart. His temperature ascended above normal and his body was as a steam of charcoal. The sweat that gushed out of his pores was insufficient to cool his blazing skin. When there was no improvement in his health, Uncle Joe advised that he should be taken to a health facility in Monrovia.

At this, Uncle Joe blew the whistle of the epidemic but it *fell on deaf ears* and the family was *stiff-necked*.

"I told them that everyone should be careful," Uncle Joe warned. "I had heard of the outbreak of Ebola in Congo and how people died.

"I know the signs and I saw them in my in-law. I told them that it was better to get tested for early treatment but they didn't listen. They were highly religious and though they could speak the light to shine, they should have applied wisdom."

Uncle Joe's advice to the family was like the east wind to the ears of a horse. Sadly, their feet were too heavy to take steps and their eyes could not capture the danger afar. Unfortunately, Ma. Fatu was not isolated from her husband and children who were placed at high risk of contracting Ebola – if she had.

The early morning of August 20, 2014 saw Mr. Stewart at the front door of his home. His nephew Christopher, and one of his daughters (Siatta) escorted him to a yellow taxi they had hired to take their father to a hospital in Monrovia. Slowly, they walked him through the doorway into the taxi.

The doors of clinics and hospitals in Kakata were closed and health workers were now hiding beneath the shadows of their roof, afraid of becoming the next meal for the deadly virus. By then, the only referral hospital in Kakata – the C.H. Rennie Hospital – was hit so severely that they started to refer patients. Onward, the family drove their father towards Monrovia. With him, were his nephew Christopher, Siatta, and his in-law Ma. Korto who was sister to Mr. Stewart's late wife. Siatta sat at the front seat with her father and the driver while Christopher and Ma. Korto sat at the back of the vehicle.

The route to Monrovia was farther than ever. Potholes and deep curves prevented the speeding of the vehicle. Slowly, it crossed the Du Bridge that ushered its passengers into Montserrado county. The commencement of the Kakata-Monrovia highway was shouldered by large rubber trees and bushes. The wind was blowing calmly. From the wet leaves, droplets of water fell.

It had rained the night before. In silence, they passed Todee and then through Number Seven – a small community along the Kakata-Monrovia highway.

On turtle's wheel, they crossed the 15-Gate checkpoint where police officers solemnly stood.

Weak, and feeble, sat Mr. Stewart, with his head resting against the front seat of the vehicle.

They drove on potholes and deep curves that pounded their hearts with grief. As they rode on, they hoped that day and the days ahead could bring them fortune; they hoped that the storm that blew rigidly over their family could soon be calm.

At long last, their vehicle set tires on the streets of Redlight that led them to the Benson Hospital in Duport Road.

The crowded market of Redlight that once welcomed strangers with its noises now embraced them in solitude. Her streets laid naked with abandoned carcasses kissing their sidewalks. This was a sign that the epidemic was real and raging.

After all the sacrifices, they finally arrived at the Benson Hospital in Duport Road. When the medical history was gathered from Mr. Stewart, he was only given an injection and was refused admittance at the Benson Hospital. It may have been that he came from a high-risk area, therefore, he was referred to the Médicins Sans Frontières (MSF) Hospital in the ELWA community.

The family did not give up but prepared for another journey to the MSF Medical facility. Upon their arrival at the MSF Hospital in ELWA, a scene of sorrow unfolded as a sign of trouble.

They were addressed aggressively by the security on guard. The security refused to allow them entry on grounds that rumors had it that an Ebola patient was aboard the vehicle. In her distress, Ma. Korto addressed the security:

"My brother, we are not fighting war," she said. "Though we are carrying a sick patient, we cannot say he has Ebola or not because we are not doctors. This is why we have come to a health facility to have our patient tested. If he has Ebola, then he can be treated. We hear on the radio every day that we should report sick patients to the hospital and that is why we have brought him here."

After confrontations and appeal, the Stewarts were finally given entry into the facility. Unfortunately, but fortunately for him, Mr. Stewart's condition seemed better than those who were admitted at the MSF health facility. People who were at the facility were living dead and only awaiting to answer the roll call of death.

One of the white doctors at the facility conducted a brief interview with Mr. Stewart, and said to him:

"You look stronger and healthier than everyone who is admitted here. You see their conditions. These people here are all awaiting death. There's no hope of survival for them and we cannot place you among them. I advise that you go back and be treated home for now."

The sad reality drove them away. With few drugs given him, Mr. Stewart and his family marched back into the taxi and headed home. Gathering hope, the family drove through the curves and potholes, back to their roots.

Patience had just lost her mother she loved best, and her heart was now turned towards her father who was left. Sadly, he too was on the path of death. The community had it that Ebola was responsible for the death of Ma. Fatu and now that her husband had fallen sick, the neighbors became skeptical of the Stewarts and avoided them. All alone, they were left, beaten by the psychological and emotional lashes that the epidemic landed on their bodies.

The clock ticked and lighting bugs turned themselves into stars – igniting sleepless and mournful nights. The wind blew colder but harder, causing dead leaves too to fall from the branches of trees. It was muddy and cold and for solution, the family knew not where to go.

At night, sorrows prevented Patience's eyes from being captured by sleep, while the cries from crickets and owls were the only melodies to which she tapped her feet.

Notwithstanding, sun rose and the daylight of August 27 actually broke because hearts too were going to be broken. On his warm bed, Mr. Stewart rested while Ma. Malah administered his medication. He was very weak and laid on a mattress in the sitting room.

"That morning," Ma. Malah recalled, "Mr. Stewart was laying in the sitting room on a mattress. Members from the church came to pray along with him and pleaded with God in devotion for his recovery. It was a home service that day, and after the service, Pastor Ernest, a member of another congregation decided to remain and offer a special prayer. Mr. Stewart rested on his back on the mattress. With their eyes closed, Pastor Ernest raised his voice in supplication to God.

"After a long prayer," Ma. Malah remembered "my in-law sat up and said to his friend Pastor Ernest: My man, leave me alone. I almost reached and you people are bothering me."

"With those words, he laid still on the mattress and closed his eyes. He didn't talk again. I called but he did not answer, I shook him but he did not wake up. Then, I knew he was dead."

That morning, death kissed Mr. Stewart's cheeks. His feet and hands were stiff and his skin cold and pale. His lips could not say a word nor his head could nod to his name. Mr. Stewart was dead and gone; for him, mourning songs began.

The wind held back the gospel of recovery for him. The shackle that knotted his spirit to life untied.

It was another teary day for the Stewarts. Exactly 17 days after death set his wife apart from him, Mr. Stewart's soul departed and joined in matrimony with her soul. Indeed, till death did they part. The roof of their home was fed with sobbing and the curtains could no longer conceal the secrets of misfortune.

The family bitterly wept and upon them, the spirits of death hastily crept. Their cries travelled through the windows of their home and brought back a troop of neighbors.

Some stood afar with hands folded while others formed nests of gossip and whispered: "I'm sure it is Ebola that killed him," said one to another. "It could be true," said another, "his wife just passed off over two weeks ago."

The scornful scene now threatened the neighbors who had interacted with the Stewarts and a handful of sympathizers that stood by. Uncle Joe again warned the family to be careful about how they cared for both the living and the dead. As for him, he was always mindful – washing his hands regularly and avoiding close contacts with those who were sick and the ones who died.

Shortly, the burial team was called and Mr. Stewart was given a safe burial.

"After the death of my mate," Uncle Joe remembered, "I brought a few buckets, chloride, and tie soap at the house for the preparation of sanitary solutions."

Uncle Joe refers to Mr. Stewart as his mate because his wife, Ma. Korto, is a sister to Ma. Fatu.

The family lamented Mr. Stewart's death and the death of his wife too. At that point, they started to be cautious but the epidemic had made its way into their family and had turned Patience into an orphan – losing both parents. Soon, other members of the family who should have given her hope started to fall sick.

Patience's distress could no longer be cheered and solitude seasoned her days and nights. After the death of Mr. Stewart and his wife, the entire family was quarantined.

Only the Stewarts were left in their big maroon home to care for themselves, only the Stewarts were left to battle the virus. At times, the health workers came and gathered statistics about their health status and provided medication.

The community members had abandoned them and bolted their entrances that lead to the home of the Stewarts. "The community people abandoned us," said Ma. Malah, "they stopped their children from visiting us and blocked the entrances from their homes that led to our yard. It was not easy."

If those who penetrated the storm and stood with the family were to be reckoned, Ma. Malah and Uncle Joe would be enlisted first. They stood their grounds, through the storms and rainfall embracing both the pain and the pleasure.

CHAPTER SIX

Siatta's Dream

August became egregious for the Stewarts. The roof that sheltered the troubled bricks and surrounded the family no longer felt like home. Tongues misplaced their taste for delicious African meals and minds no longer caught happy memories of the past. But the storm was just about to blow. A few days after the death of their parents, the warning was but a scary dream. Patience's elder sister Siatta had a dream:

"I was walking alone on a narrow path to a large building. The road was dark and narrow and the sound of a large crowd directed the steps of my feet into the distance ahead. As I walked, fear gripped me and goosebumps plastered my skin. I moved faster and darkness filled the empty pathway that laid behind me. The closer I came to this large building, the louder the crowd sounded and the path that laid behind me became dark.

"Suddenly, I came to a point where I could see the crowd – some sitting and others standing. Among them was my late mother. She was cooking and it appeared they were attending a conference. Shortly, my late father arrived and his late mother and one of her friends began to welcome him. They give him a room to stay. When I saw this, I started walking into the building. The entrance of the building had about three stairs. I climbed the first two, and was about to climb the third stirs when the skies above my head and the ground beneath my feet started spinning. When I attempted to climb the third stirs, I heard a very loud voice, one that I've never heard:
'This is not your time, go back,' the voice sounded.

"The sound of the voice was so loud that my ears could not withstand it. Then blew a very strong wind that threw me out of the doorway. I fell on my back, flat to the ground. I stared around me and I saw people – some standing and others sitting with bundles beside them. Some of them I knew and others I didn't. Soon, the voice started to direct me out of the place.

'There are three gates along this road," it said. "Do not go through any of these gates.'

"I continued moving. I crossed the first gate and when I arrived at the second gate, I saw two securities. Then the voice said to me 'When they ask you, tell them my father, my father sent me.'

"For sure, when I arrived at the second gate, the securities asked 'Who sent you?' and then I said to them: 'Rev. Molley F. Stewart sent me.'

"At this, they pointed their fingers towards a bushy path. Then I walked towards the path and started travelling through. The road was grassy and ropes from plants held me back. I was cut by saw grasses and pricked by thorns. I struggled my way through and reached the third gate.

"At the third gate, I was directed by the voice to a white house. The voice warned that I should not enter the house. I could not see the roof of this white house because it was covered with clouds. I escaped the house and was passing at the back when I saw a white car. The voice said to me that the owner of the white house was the owner of the white car. Again, the voice warned that I should not allow the man to see me.

'He is a wicked person,' the voice said, 'If he sees you, he would not allow you to get back.'

"I hid myself and sneaked by the house into a dark and bushy pathway. Beneath my feet, dried sticks and leaves plastered the ground and made scaring sounds as I stepped on. The bush around me was very high. Branches of trees hindered the light from the skies. So I crept slowly through the bush and struggled my way out.

"Suddenly, I arrived at a muddy swamp where I came across a small stream. The water way was but the only route out; yet I was afraid to pass through. I tapped my left feet into the water to test its depth. I was frightened that I could have sunk deep within. My dream felt real and I became more scared. To be sure that the water was not deep enough, I broke a piece of stick from a nearby tree and dipped it in the water. I dipped the stick slowly into the water and half of it was swallowed when it reached the bottom of the stream. I discovered that it was not deep enough so I slowly stepped and walked through the water that held me at knee level.

As I walked through, the dried leaves and sticks that floated hitched all over my dress. Slowly, I crossed the stream and came across a dry pathway. I navigated my way through the thorns and high grassland. I parted the bush with my hands. Saw grasses and thorns pierced my body; roots and limbs held my feet, yet I kept moving forward.

"As I struggled to navigate my way out, I finally I saw myself out of the bush, at the front of our home. Out of a sudden, I woke up from bed and found that it was a dream.

"When I woke up, I recognized that the dress I wore in my dream was the dress I slept in that night and the sandal on my feet was one that I had."

When Siatta woke up, the cries of owls and chirps from crickets directed fear down her spines.

The bats that danced before the stars deepened her scars. She thought she was dead. She began to pinch herself to feel the presence of life. No, she was not dead but alive.

The reality of what embraced her was the calamity of death and a disease that escorted her family – one at a time – to the great beyond.

As the rain descended upon the rooftop, she yearned for the blessings of a new day – maybe another miserable day.

Soon, daylight crept through flashes of lightning and the clouds that hung over Kakata broke into a new day. Siatta's dream was but a sign that the tides were just beginning to rise and the clock on the wall was ticking anti-clockwise.

In August, Kakata stood still as it mourned over five nurses who were snatched away from the C.H. Rennie Hospital – the only referral hospital in Kakata – along with other prominent citizens.

CHAPTER SEVEN

Ebola Kills Three Stewarts

Like wildfire, death spread throughout, from the city nooks to the highway, and to every hut and duplex planted on the soil of Liberia. Even Patience's cousin Jackson also lost his best friend James to the epidemic.

Onward, one after the other, each member of Patience's household began to fall ill with similar symptoms – red eyes, rashes on skin, and high fever. At that point, it was clear that what seemed to have been an ordinary headache was now the dreadful disease everyone feared.

Uncle Joe now took a stand and tied wisdom beneath his belt. He rolled up his sheaths to prevent an entire generation from erasing from the pages of history. He ordered the preparation of warm solution containing tie soap and chloride for the washing of hands, dishes, floors, door knobs, and other things that were frequently touched. Washing hands became a tradition in the home of the Stewarts.

The fingers of the epidemic flipped the pages of August away, and unfolded the chapters of September. Annie, Patience's aunt from her father's lineage had already fallen critically ill; showing varying symptoms of Ebola such as red eyes, vomiting, weakness and high fever. Her body's immunity could no longer withstand the physical and emotional tension that accompanied the disease. Slowly, she succumbed to the scripts of the epidemic.

On 1st September 2014, arrangements were made to take Annie to the ETU. At first, a commercial taxi driver was contacted to take her to the hospital. Upon his arrival, silence and fear tortured his instinct and it appeared to him that something was wrong. The taxi driver decided to place a high price on the trip because it seemed like he was risking his life due to the fact that the family was known to be affected by Ebola. When negotiation ended in deadlock, the taxi driver turned his back against the family, entered his vehicle and sped out of the yard. The mud that emitted behind the vehicle beat the hearts of the Stewarts and drove solitude down their veins. To whom now will they turn to? Where do they now find help?

Alternatively, Ezekiel and Christopher made another arrangement for a vehicle to take their aunt

Annie to the ETU in Monrovia. Soon, another driver arrived. That morning, it appeared as if it was about to rain. Dark clouds and thunderstorm sounded a warning of danger. Droplets of gossips fell from the faucet of the community members as some of them peeped through their windows to watch.

Aunty Annie was persuaded to board the taxi. Weak and feeble, she dragged her wounded body slowly into the yellow taxi. Her nephews Ezekiel and Christopher went along with her that morning. It was another scene of sorrow. Great fear engulfed the Stewarts again and through their veins, pupped fear and pain. In tears, the other members of the family bade her goodbye.

The taxi drove slowly through the narrow and dusty community roads and through the main streets of Kakata. In jet plane speed, it dashed on potholes and swung through narrow curves. On the seat of the taxi, Aunty Annie struggled to gasp for the fragrance of life, vomiting and sweating profusely. Like the angry tides of the Atlantic Ocean, her temperature arose and her body shivered like a nervous kid.

Upon arrival at 15th Gate along the Kakata-Monrovia highway, she poured out her last breath like a warm glass of tea and died. Her remains were buried along with others in a mass grave and for her, there's not much of a memory.

While the Stewarts lamented the loss of their parents and aunt, Ezekiel – Patience's half-brother and Christopher had fallen sick.

Ezekiel now started to show grave symptoms of Ebola: vomiting, weakness and rashes on his skin. He lived just a stone throw away from their family home. He had come in close contact with his late mother and aunt. He strongly disbelieved in the reality of the epidemic and thought it to be a spiritual attack against his family.

As the family pierced through the dense of time and tension, they made frantic efforts to have Ezekiel and Christopher treated or taken to the ETU but all efforts turned fatal.

It saddened them to have been informed by the C.H. Rennie Hospital that the hospital itself was wounded and needed attention. The only ambulance which was available at the time was under repair. Many of their doctors too were sick, and some had abandoned their duties. The arrangement of the ambulance was like gold dust – very difficult to obtain.

If it took a strong person to arrange an ambulance by then, whose feet were strong among them? Whose mind was peaceful as rivers to think twice? Whose fear was fearless enough to pick a fight?

Although Uncle Joe confronted Ezekiel and his cousin Christopher to seek medical attention, the unattainability of an ambulance at the time, caused them to find solution of their own. In the wisdom of their ignorance, Christopher hires a motorcycle and attempts to escape with Ezekiel one early morning in September to a traditional herbalist.

Christopher perceives that the banner of sickness that swings over his family is spiritual and could be removed by a native doctor. By then, he had already visited a shrine and was pierced thrice on his left arm as a mark of protection against the evil.

It's early morning, September 5 or so. The dew falls from the roofs of homes and the petals of flowers unclutter to warm themselves with the light of the rising sun. Christopher and Ezekiel head to an herbalist in a small village bordering Kakata.

News reaches the health team of their plans and shortly, the health team intercepts them along the way and brings them back home to be quarantined again.

Amidst the calamities, Christopher refuses to bow to the direction of the rising tides.

It is the cool of the evening. Again, Christopher hides under dark clouds and flees with his cousin Ezekiel to a native doctor. They arrive, panting and shivering; temperature blazing like a furnace and eyes red as blood.

"Sit down my children," the native doctor welcomes them. "I'm hearing that people are dying plenty in town and you don't want to die that's why you are here. But the gods of my ancestors have never failed, and will never fail" the native doctor assures them.

"Ahem-ahem," the native doctor clears his throat. He throws a few gamble seeds and steadily gaze at them for a while. "Here, have this! Rub this chalk early in the morning after bathing. In the evening after bathing, rub it again before going to bed," the native doctor continues. Someone in your family is responsible for this but they will not succeed."

Christopher and Ezekiel spent their night in the 'sick bush', burning with fever. The hut built from tiny rattan and plastered with mud feels safer for them but it's not their home. It's somewhere in a village, so the cries of night creatures are different. That night, the native doctor performed several rituals and the next morning, the message sent through the bell of the town crier woke them up. In one bundle, they knotted themselves and headed for Kakata.

Though Christopher and Ezekiel sought a solution from the native doctor, Ezekiel's condition worsened and he was isolated in a room along with his wife. Twelve days after he lost his aunt and endured the pain, the 13th of September brought upon Ezekiel's head a bundle too heavy to bear.

It is 5:00 AM and Ezekiel lays in the room with his girlfriend Tina.

"I am very thirsty' Ezekiel grunts. Please help me with water. Inside here is too hot and I cannot breathe properly."

Hastily, his fiancée Tina gives him a cup of

water to drink and brings him outside on their porch to feed on the cold air of the morning. Ezekiel takes off his shirt and on the mat, he lays, resting his head on a piece of cushion.

He drinks the water and places the cup beside him, on the floor. His fiancée stands beside him, more worried than ever. Even the water Ezekiel gulpes seemes not cold enough to quench the flames that glows within him. By then, his organs and system were being squashed by the disease and like a blazing charcoal, his temperature arose.

His eyes as red as ripe pepper and rashes plastered the covering of his body.

Ezekiel grunts silently, his words chock. He feels miserable within, turning sidewise, from one end of the mat to another. After a moment, he quivers, and lays motionless.

"Meho!" "Meho," his girlfriend calls his nickname. Ezekiel could not speak a word nor hummed. The pupils in his eyes were stable and it appeared as though he was looking amazingly at a ghost. His hands stiff and so were his feet.

Panting and crying, Ezekiel's girlfriend takes up heels and runs at the family house to inform the other members of the severity of his illness. Only upon their arrival did they discover that Ezekiel had died.

It was September 13, another day. Choruses of mourning poured out of the home of the Stewarts. They dashed themselves against the floors and slammed doors in astonishment. Eyes were swollen from cries from the past, so they were tried to spew tears in the present.

Shortly, the burial team was called to carry the remains of Ezekiel, and with the knowledge of his family, he was taken; dust-to-dust, ashes-to-ashes. To him, death was appointed once; and it was not his end but a means to Heaven's land.

From the signs and symptoms that showed up in Ezekiel, it was obvious that Ebola was the cause of his death. If this was so, it might have been the cause of death for the ones who had died before and the ones who had fallen sick.

Now, hell broke loose for an already shattered family. Too many cross-interactions had occurred and to most of them, the virus had already spread. Now, the hands of fear held Patience so tightly that even a tickle on her ribs was enough to make her cry rather than laugh.

Uncle Joe mustered courage and seriously warned every member of the family:

"If anyone is sick, do not touch them," he said. If you feel sick, inform me so that I can arrange for you to be treated at the ETU. It will be better that you are treated at the ETU to recover than dying here one at a time."

Already, Christopher, Patience's cousin was sickening and laid in a deplorable condition. The death of his cousin Ezekiel psychologically whipped his mind. Engraved on his wall, was one blurred word; one he could not tell was 'LIFE' or 'DEATH'. In hemlock wine, he dipped his faith as Hades was gladly determining his fate. The health team had self-quarantined Christopher and cautioned the family to avoid close contact with him.

The following morning, September 14, 2014, Christopher fell severely sick. His eyes red like the flames from a bonfire and his body burned like a piece of dry wood that was lit. He was isolated alone in his room.

On that morning, Christopher murmured about his health. Within the house, other relatives stood outside watching, while others soughed solutions.

"I'm thirsty, please give me water to drink," Christopher pleaded.

Because of the advice from the health team, no one could go closer to Christopher. A bottle was filled with water and threw at him. With his elbow bent and mouth opened wide, he poured the bottle of water deep into his throat.

It seemed like his thirst could not have been quenched by water, or maybe, an iceberg inserted into his stomach could have appeased his thirst and stabilized his temperature.

Christopher felt miserable inside. He complained about weakness, headache and pain. He was so uncomfortable that he started to roll on the floor. Some of his family members stood by and watched him roll from one corner of the room to another, gasping for air and fighting for life. Things fell off the table as he fought from one end of the room to another. Like the valley of dry bones, a loud noise arose from the room.

At that moment, Christopher stood face-to-face with death. His arms weak to lift a fist, his legs feeble to take their stand and to death, he was about to surrender.

In tears, Uncle Joe stood by watching as Christopher wrestled with death on the stage of life.

"I watched my nephew fight from one end of the room to another," Uncle Joe recalled. I watched him die like a movie thriller. I could not withstand the cries and screams from his brothers and sisters.

I could not withstand the family dashing themselves on the floor and against the dust; yet, I kept my distance and helped them to keep theirs.

I'm a man, but at that moment, I lost my bravery. I burst into tears as I watched my nephew die in pain. After fighting for almost five minutes, the noise in the room seized and he laid in peace, still on the floor.

"Christopher. Christopher! I called him but he didn't answer. Then I knew his soul had departed his body. I knew he had given up his ghost."

Indeed, Christopher was thirsty, thirsty not for

cold water but for the cold hands of death; thirsty for the great beyond rather than the land where he was born. As Christopher laid quietly on the floor, the health team was called.

After a few minutes, they arrived and confirmed his death and immediately, Christopher was given a safe burial.

CHAPTER EIGHT

Patience Contracts Ebola

At the end of September, Tina, Ezekiel's fiancée, had fallen severely sick and was taken at the ELWA ETU in Monrovia where she was tested positive for Ebola. A few days after, her family lost total communication with her. The nine-month old pregnant woman was expecting a baby when the epidemic held her hands.

All efforts to reach out to her turned fatal. No one knew what was going on. If she was dead or alive, no one could tell, no one knew except the Almighty.

Uncle Joe recalled: "Few days after Tina's arrival at the center, we lost total communication with her. I contacted friends and family I knew who were working at the center but they promised to get back to me if they had any information.

Days after, I was informed by one of the nurses who I knew that Tina had died along with her unborn child. When I heard this, I broke down.

That child never had a chance to see the light of day, not even for once."

At that time, the government of Liberia had issued an executive order for the cremation of affected bodies and her body was burned flames-to-wind, flesh-to-ashes. As for her, not even a memory of her grave remains nor her ashes kept for remembrance.

Must it always be dishonor before death? For goodness' sake, even if death must come, must it not come with honor? Members of the Stewarts were not dying honorably. Their bodies were labeled 'Danger' and the normal burial ritual according to their tradition and religion were not performed. Now, death was victorious over the Stewarts: "*O death, where is thy sting? O grave, where is thy victory?*"

An endless string of emotional trauma entangled itself around Patience's body. Against pain and sorrows she dashed her soul.

Patience's mind became a cage for stray thoughts that pierced her heart with misery. Her ears rejected the sound of siren that reminded her of the tragedy of the past, and the ones to come.

The Stewarts were now sailing through storms and in their misfortune, an opulence of health was nowhere to be found. On bended knees, they offered countless supplications because the ones who won bread for their family had already become bread for the epidemic. Unfolding days threatened their family with misfortune. Music was no longer food for Patience's frightening soul, and for the gospel she yearned. 'God why me?' was the question she daily asked.

It seemed her prayers from the past and the ones she offered at the time were falling on sandy grounds. She was just 16 years old, and in the eighth grade. The epidemic had forced her into becoming an orphan and amongst thorns and weeds, her expectations were thrown.

The mysterious death of members of the Stewarts now became a concern of the public. It was then Uncle Joe became more proactive and started to engage NGOs and the Ministry of Health to get members of his family tested and treated if they were Ebola positive.

Several members of the family were already showing symptoms of the virus. In an effort to save the family, Siatta also contacted a friend who worked with the International Medical Corpse (IMC) to assist some members of the family seek medical treatment at the ETU in Gbarnga.

It was Friday afternoon, October 3, 2014. Thick droplets of rain poured down from the clouds and made horrifying noise on the rooftop.

Lightning and thunderstorm warned the family against the calamity of the epidemic.

Rain-rain come down, potter-potter go up' was the theme song that Liberian kids sing during the rainy season. But with the sorrows brought upon families by that rainy season, little children forgot its theme song because the older folks were not timely in preparing their daily meals.

In the heavy rain, Uncle Joe was arranging an ambulance to take a few members of his family to the Redemption Hospital.

October 3, 2014 was a cold and rainy day. Anyhow, Uncle Joe slapped his fatigued body against the rain in search of an ambulance to take Patience and the others to an ETU. He was soaking wet, with water dripping down his clothes, down to the soles of his feet. His teeth were whacking, his body shivered and cold bumps decorated the surface of his skin.

Even at that, Uncle Joe didn't give up in his quest to discover a solution. He dialed one number after another, he travelled from one place to another, and asked one question after another; something he believed would unearth a remedy. Finally, during one of his calls, Uncle Joe bumped into Mrs. Mai Urey, Chief Executive Officer of Urey Foundation – an organization that was providing medical assistance to families affected by the epidemic.

An ambulance was finally provided by the Foundation and arrived that evening. The cold wind blew the leaves of wet trees as the blinking lights and emergency siren of the ambulance became a force of attraction for bystanders. This compelled many of the neighbors to tear their curtains and peep through the windows of their homes.

With folded hands and winkling eyes, they watched Patience, Darius and Hellen slowly marched into the ambulance. The health workers assigned with the ambulance sprayed chlorine solution as they marched on, into the ambulance.

One after another, the ambulance swallowed them up. Hellen who was pregnant at the time, was the one given much attention. The lights of the ambulance were blinking, its siren sounded louder and strained the ears of the Stewarts. At high speed, it drove out of the yard and its siren slowly faded in a distance.

Uncle Joe was standing at the eve of the house watching. He was soaking wet and stared amazingly as the splash of mud behind the ambulance bade goodbye. The rain became heavier, and onward to the Redemption Hospital, the ambulance took off. With his arms folded, Uncle Joe stood staring at the droplets of rain that beat the soil and dug up mud. As the scenes of the past and the present danced on the stage of his mind, he nodded his head in rejection. The rain was so heavy that he could not see the houses across the street.

As he stood, he hoped that the hospital would bring redemption to the ill, as the name 'Redemption Hospital' implies.

As the ambulance drove on, Patience held on tight to the chair she sat on. To her, it seemed like a fly more than a ride. As the speed of the ambulance increased, her stomach quivered from the rocking and swinging. She was the oldest among them, and she felt responsible.

She looked after the little ones along the way. She used the cellphone provided by her Uncle to update him about their health conditions and the distance they had covered.

The Kakata-Monrovia highway was not a paved one and she felt like throwing out. While traveling, along the Kakata-Monrovia highway, what should have been an emergency spun into an uncertainty. The ambulance that was carrying Patience, Darius and Hellen had a breakdown at the Careys Burg community.

News soon reached Uncle Joe and he became worried. Troubled by the news, he made several phone calls from one point to another but things appeared not to have been working.

The evening sun had sunk deep in the belly of the ocean that bounded the southwestern borders of Liberia. A dark cloud filled with rain hung over the nation. The stars were lining up in the cloud, and the croaks from swamp frogs stirred fear in Patience's heart.

Until 9:00 PM, all efforts exerted by Uncle Joe to arrange another ambulance for his nieces and nephew turned fatal. Patience and her siblings sat in the ambulance in pursuit of a solution. She continuously rang her Uncle's telephone to inform him about their misfortune. As Uncle Joe dropped the phone line with Patience, he too rang the lines of health authorities. Patience and the kids were hungry, but could not leave an inch out of the ambulance because of their condition.

After several calls among Patience, Uncle Joe and Health Workers, another ambulance was sent from the Redemption Hospital to take Patience and the other kids. Again, another journey began, from the rocky road of the Kakata-Monrovia highway to the paved road of Somalia Drive and onward through the streets of New Kru town, they finally arrived at the Redemption Hospital.

It was about 11:00 PM, October 3, 2014 when they arrived. Upon arrival, the ambulance driver who took them locked them up in the ambulance and they were left at the mercy of the virus. Patience again reached out to her cell phone and dialed her Uncle's number again. After several phone calls, they received help and were taken into the facility.

As they were entering the hospital, bodies shouldered the sides of the hallway through which they entered – some severely ill and some dead. Vomits and toilets plastered the floor beneath their feet.

At some point, they had to jump over one of the bodies that laid along the way. Despite how deplorable conditions were, Patience kept the faith. She held on to life though death was knocking at her doors. Finally, she was directed in one of the rooms in the hospital and the other kids were taken to separate rooms. There, she was to spend a night, sleeping on a bed without beddings.

Things had fallen apart because many health workers refused to play their part. Most of the beddings were messed up and there was no one to do laundry work.

All alone, Patience was left in the hospital room, with no one to care for her. Most of the nurses had abandoned their duties and the sick – especially those who came from high-risk zones, like Patience. Inscribed on the walls of the hospital was the Florence Nightingale Pledge:

"I solemnly pledge myself before God and in the presence of this assembly, to pass my life in purity and to practice my profession faithfully. I will abstain from whatever is deleterious and mischievous, and will not take or knowingly administer any harmful drug. I will do all in my power to maintain and elevate the standard of my profession, and will hold in confidence all personal matters committed to my keeping and all family affairs coming to my knowledge in the practice of my calling. With loyalty will I endeavor to aid the physician in his work, and devote myself to the welfare of those committed to my care."

This pledge is often recited at graduation/pinning ceremonies for nurses. But at this juncture, it seemed as if nurses had forgotten this pledge. It seemed as if the Ebola virus had blotted out the lines of the pledge from the minds of many health workers.

Only a few were willing to lay down their lives and keep their commitment to this pledge; only a few were devoting themselves to the welfare of those committed to their care.

At Redemption Hospital, Patience was left alone to care for herself. She became confused by the scenes her eyes begot, and immediately, she called Uncle Joe and cried on the telephone:

"I'm scared! They've placed us amongst dead bodies. Vomits and feces are all on the floor and there's no one to care for us."

Uncle Joe too was confused and didn't know what to do. The night was dark as black and it was about 2:00 AM. Those who could have rendered assistance were all asleep, and he too was restless and wanted to catch a nap.

"Patience," Uncle Joe said to her, "turn your face to the wall! Forget about those people, they are dead and will not do anything to you."

Patience did as he said. Like a doughnut, she folded herself, faced the wall and closed her eyes tightly. That night, the road to dream's land was narrow and slippery. She thought about Hellen and Darius, she thought about those old terrifying memories and she thought about herself.

Uncomfortable as she was, Patience found no pleasure in sleep; yet, sleep came and took her for a ride during the deepest span of the night.

It was October 4, 2014. On that fateful Saturday morning, it was only the sound of the rising tides of the beach that reminded Patience of a new day; a day that came like a rushing wind.

It was another horrible; yet promising day. Those who had been carried at the Redemption Hospital were not given much attention. The ambiance of the hospital was one that did not assure anyone of life. On an aura of death, patients sniffed.

Most of them were being transferred to either the John F. Kennedy Hospital in Monrovia or the ELWA Hospital. The government of Liberia and her partners were now preparing a few treatment centers around the country.

It was about 9:00 that morning and Patience had not eaten anything. She was hungry, and thirsty too, and there was no one to attend to her. Her only means of crying out for help was through her cellphone. She reached out for her phone and called Uncle Joe. She complained about how she was dying from both the disease and hunger. She complained about how there were no nurses available to help them; she complained about how she slept without beddings and how the scent of vomits and feces had worsened her condition. And at this, Uncle Joe turned to others who were in the health sector for help including a man he only identified as Appleton.

"Because of the countless number of calls I received from my niece, I was sometimes confused. That morning when I stabilized, I remembered that I had a brother who was working with the burial team that I could reach out to. Then I called Sam and pleaded with him to ensure that my people are transferred to a better place. Immediately Sam started arrangements and assured me that he was going to have them transferred and he did as promised."

CHAPTER NINE

Patience Transfered to an ETU

On Sunday evening, October 5, 2014, Patience, Hellen, Darius and other victims were transferred to the ELWA Treatment Unit to be tested. She didn't carry much clothes except a small bag that she held in her hand with just a few undies. Darius and Hellen were too frail. Their bodies blazed in fever so greatly that Patience's heart pounded in fear. Upon arrival at the ELWA ETU, they all were taken into separate locations and their blood samples were collected.

Feeble and weak, Patience sat beneath a tent at the ELWA ETU and awaited her results. For hours she waited, changing sitting position from one style to another. She sat alone with her elbow resting over her knees, her cheek seated in her right palm, and her head bent over. Patience fell asleep for a while and then woke up. Her temperature blazing hot but not surprising; her body feverish but not shivering. To her, it seemed as though a band of soldiers marched in her stomach – it pained her. Her heart too beat louder than the hand bell of a town crier and all she needed at the time was some rest.

After sitting for hours, the clock ticked 21:00 GMT. As she stared in a distance, a lady walked up to her and others who awaited their results. She was a health worker, well suited in a white PPE. Her face decorated with a shield that only her eyes were seen and her name tag pointed out from her chest. She stood with a register in her hand and gazed above the heads of those who sat before her. One after another, names were called, then, "Patience Stewart." The lady calling the names paused for a while. Patience's heart pounded the loudest. After few seconds, the lady continued her roll call. Approximately 27 persons were called when the lady stopped. "You all are positive," she said "and you will have to follow me this way," she pointed towards her left. "Do not take anything that you brought with you, I repeat, do not take anything that you brought."

Patience along with others who were called, were directed to a new location to stay. It seemed not like the usual home where beds were made up and food seated majestically upon dining tables; it seemed not like the friendly Liberian neighborhood where one could visit a friend and have a conversation. No, the ETU was a place of isolation – in fact, it was an academy that prepared victims for the 'hereafter'. Patience walked sadly into the tent and crept slowly into a lonely bed.

There, she rested on her back with her face upward, stirring at the top of the canopy. Her mind navigated between the scenes that paved the path for her arrival and an illusion of how the future could present itself. It was about 11:00 PM and the stars watched over their tents in sorrows.

Though darkness grew thicker and the hour hand on the wall clock pointed to the zero hour, Patience's eyes could not catch her midnight flight. Upon her descended a noxious feeling. Minutes later, she started to throw out.

Her body oozed with heat like a piece of charcoal that had been lit. She became weak; taunted and hunted by the horrible scenes of calamity she experienced. It appeared as if she had been beaten severely. Her restless body laid like a dead dog on the bed, and her eyes burned from the tears and hot temperature of her body.

Finally, after her mind drove her through the horrible scenes of the days before, it rested and landed her far asleep.

As the clock ticked and the cold raged, a new day broke. Then came Monday, October 6, 2014. That morning, Patience woke up to the death of a girl whose bed laid next to hers.

The corpse of the girl was sprayed and wrapped like a piece of sandwich bread in an alumni foil. Those who came to collect the carcass were suited in their PPEs and face shields that none could identify them. Into a white zip bag, they placed the lifeless body of the girl and carried her away – one person holding the head and another at the feet. Patience wasn't afraid anymore. It was something she had gotten used to. Fear was her friend and the dead wasn't a foe to her anymore.

Naomi, the girl who laid next to Patience whispered, "My dear, be strong oh, hmm, this area is a place to help yourself. Every day someone dies here. Just pray that the ones who will die in the coming days will not be you."

Naomi introduced herself to Patience and so did Patience. At the moment, they became friends and kept the company of one another. They had a long conversation sharing their experience about what they went through. Later, Naomi said to Patience:

"Can you put strength in yourself so we can take a shower?" Naomi asked Patience.

"*Yes,*" Patience reluctantly replied. Her soul struggled to drag her weak body off the bed but at long last, she dashed off the bed and went to the shower. Thereafter, Patience and Naomi hopped back into their separate beds that sat one to another.

Suddenly, Naomi's phone began to ring. She reached out for her phone that laid at the head of her bed. She punched the answered button and placed it to her ears. Naomi had received a call from one of her relatives who was checking on the status of her health. Patience stirred at her as she responded on the phone:

"I am trying oh, I will be okay by God's Grace."

Minutes later, Naomi's voice faded beneath the telephone as though she was falling asleep.

"*Hello... Hello...*," the person who was calling sounded. The phone had slipped from Naomi's hand and was now laying on the bed beside her right ear.

Seconds later, the phone started ringing again. Naomi laid in silence and did not make an attempt to reconnect.

Then, Patience called out to another patient across Naomi's bed: "Sister, the phone is ringing and Naomi is not picking. What happened?" Patience asked.

At Patience's call, the lady reached out to Naomi and stirred at her in awe. After a moment, she nodded her head and whispered: "She's dead. The nurses will come and carry her body."

It was true that Naomi had died. The nurses came and confirmed her death. They wrapped Naomi's body in a white zip bag and the burial team was ready to take her off. With one person at the head and one at the feet, they marched slowly and disappeared in a distance.

Patience was shocked as she stared in disbelief. She wondered: 'How could a friend leave without saying goodbye? Why will someone who prepares for death encourage others about life?"

Patience felt no sorrow when Naomi died, she was used to sorrow. She had tasted the most delicious meal that sorrow had to offer.

The 7th of October brought tasteless memories to Patience's mind – memories of how her father would sit on their porch on Sunday to listen to his small black radio and prepare his sermons; memories of how she would assist her mother to cook on Sunday morning. Now that her family was baptized in pain and death had untied her parents' string, hope for Patience was lost. She was now alone, praying for her own recovery; with no appetite to eat and no peace to sleep.

As the warm sun crept through the grieving clouds of Liberia, days broke and so did hearts to the death news of relatives and friends. In the land, there was no family, no group of friends, no community and no county that was yet to feel the pinch of the beast. The wind blew through every home on the soil of Liberia. Cries of mourning were heard from dawn to sundown and songs of morning birds no longer sounded sweet in the ears of daughters and sons.

For Patience, life in isolation was different; something she had no alternative to. She embraced her new home and a new lifestyle.

She was fed at least three times daily and administered drugs twice as she was fed. The scent of medication perfumed the air so much that it became partially uncomfortable for Patience's breath. After a few days, it felt good to breathe.

The truck loads of tablets that were administered daily had much effect on patients that even the scent of urine and sweat smelled like drugs.

Sadly, every day that broke took the life of at least a soul. Day-to-day, bodies were carried off in white zip bags to be cremated. Since August that year to the end, death continued to lash families with pain, and caused them to weep; if not for days but for months. Though people were dying at the tick of the clock, the epidemic never appeared to be seizing. As bodies were carried outside for cremation, those tested positive of Ebola were admitted to their beds.

October 5 was the worst day that Patience recalled at the ELWA ETU. Since then, she embraced the sorrows of death that life seemed to offer. Cries and grunting now sounded like the top song on her music playlist. The scent of different tablets was now smelling like a bunch of roses. For her, she tasted death and munched on sorrows. Being an orphan made her feel dead and she thought there was no need to fear death. To hell, she had been and back and now, born-again as a brave child.

Then and onward, many of those who arrived along with Patience at the ETU, and those whom she met had been wiped away by the dreadful disease; except an elderly woman – Ma. Esther.

Ma. Esther was a neighbor to Patience. Patience shared pieces of her story with Ma. Esther and as a neighbor, they built a cordial relationship daily.

Patience describes Ma. Esther as a slim lady with dark-skin; a lady who wraps her arms around the world. Her black eyes fitted neatly in their sockets and winked with hope. Her straight short black hair was plaited downward – probably, since her arrival at the ETU, she had never had a chance to change the style of her hair. Her sharp voice made her a good singer and her faith in God was a beak of hope for Patience. Ma. Esther was from Caldwell, a small settlement on the Bushrod Island in Liberia.

"Ma. Esther became my mother," Patience recalled. "Morning and evening, she led me in devotion and encouraged me that I was going to survive. Her statement of courage brought revival to me and her songs of worship to God gradually revived my soul.

I remembered, Ma. Esther always recited Psalm 118:17 to me – 'I shall not die but live to declare the works of the Lord'. I will never forget this scripture until I die. Though my biological mother was dead, I felt that I had another mother.

Gradually, Patience's faith grew stronger, and her hope no longer marched on the pavements of the past. Ma. Esther cheered up the empathy of her soul daily and fed her mind with stories of great men of faith – like Job. Increasingly, Patience's strength grew stronger and gradually, like a healing wound, she began to recover. She started to feel the kiss of life again. She started to inhale the fragrance of hope again.

Fortunately, but Sadly, Ma. Esther was declared Ebola-free and discharged. The day of her departure came and unfolded an emotional scene for her new daughter. Patience sat on her bed and folded her arms. She watched Ma. Esther gathered her belongings.

Her chin quivered melancholy and her eyes steadily blinked. Tears filled the corners of her eyes and solitude invaded her heart.

Ma. Esther zipped her bundles, bade Patience farewell and unfolded pieces of advice:

"My child, I am leaving but I am leaving God with you. Please take care of yourself. Soon, you will be wearing my shoes. Every long rope has an end and your stay here will one day end."

And so was it. That day, Ma. Esther was discharged. Her departure was a sign that the storm was subsiding and the rising tides that once beat the shores of West Africa were slowly bowing. Untold stories were now becoming stepping stones for survivors of the worst Ebola epidemic in history. Nearly 10,000 souls wrestled with the epidemic, out of which approximately 5,000 stooped to death.

The ones who escaped the clause of the epidemic navigated their way into a dangerous paradise characterized by discriminations and deceptions.

CHAPTER TEN

Patience Declared Ebola-Free

Days flipped faster than the pages of an unread chapter. Patience was lonely because her companion – Ma. Esther – was discharged from her hospital bed and integrated back into her community.

Now, Patience was looking forward to the coming of new and brighter days, and like Ma. Esther, she was hoping to be free one day. She was hoping to swallow her favorite fufu and soup instead of bitter pills. She was hoping to smell the scent of morning roses rather than the odor of antibiotics and vomits. Although she had grown stronger, and the scars that decorated her mind were gradually healing, she hoped to taste freedom soon. She hoped to gaze upon a scene of congregation and testify about her escape away from death. Until then, she sat at the edge of her lonely bed dashing pills down the gutter of her throat.

At that time, things were gradually improving and only a fewer number of patients were being admitted to hospital beds. The headlines of the print and electronic media were sounding better than before, and the number of cases reported were steadily declining.

Episodes of tragedy were being fastened beneath the belts of many families, and it was obvious that when the dust settled, only the strong were going to survive, only the brave were going to testify.

Notwithstanding, Patience endured the yoke of the epidemic and after the storms were silent, she opened her arms to embrace the gospel she long awaited – the good news of being Ebola-free.

When dawn unfolded a few weeks into October 2014, Patience inhaled an aura of courage, life and freedom. She was finally declared Ebola-free, certificated, and discharged on October 18, 2014.

A great sense of delight awaited her. On that day, comfort danced with Patience on her lonely stage. Joy painted her face with smiles and marched her soul through the aisle of life. For her, it seemed like a dream come through. She literally marched on a red carpet. The evening sun cuddled the surface of her skin and the friendly sea breeze gladly blew her dress forward; celebrating her freedom as she walked outside of her tent.

A vehicle was parked along the road awaiting her. With a joyful heart, she climbed into the vehicle and it slowly drove through the compounds of the hospital; then, out on the main road.

For the first time in weeks, she was able to gaze upon a scene of the crowd and inhale the freshness of the natural air she once missed. She sat at the front seat and stirred out through the window. Fresh air caressed her skin and her eyes again gazed upon lively scenes. A sense of anxiety wrapped itself around her body and she felt a cause to live on.

The vehicle she rode beat the moving traffic and arrived at the ELWA Junction. Upon arrival at the Junction, Patience was indecisive about which way to go.

"Left," she said to the driver and then, "No, Straight". She realized that she had to go to her sister Margret at Parker's Paint – a small community in the city of Paynesville bordering the Redlight Market. On and on, they drove through the lonely streets of Paynesville. The streets that were once crowded with strangers were now experiencing isolation. In the comfort of the seat of the car, Patience found peace for a while. As the driver slowly drove on, she imagined how happy her sister would be receiving her, she imagined the joy that her presence would unfold.

CHAPTER ELEVEN

Patience Reunites with Her Family

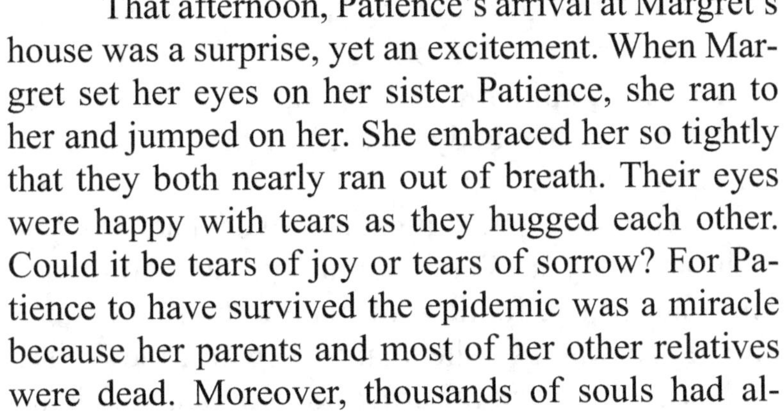

That afternoon, Patience's arrival at Margret's house was a surprise, yet an excitement. When Margret set her eyes on her sister Patience, she ran to her and jumped on her. She embraced her so tightly that they both nearly ran out of breath. Their eyes were happy with tears as they hugged each other. Could it be tears of joy or tears of sorrow? For Patience to have survived the epidemic was a miracle because her parents and most of her other relatives were dead. Moreover, thousands of souls had already stooped to the screams of death; and hundreds were in line awaiting death.

It felt good reuniting with her family again. It felt lovely waking up to the crows of roosters and falling asleep to mid-night conversations. Instead of tearing quarantine tents apart and benching with a broken heart, it felt good tearing the curtains and watching the stars dance in dark clouds.

Now that Patience was back into the community, her life after being quarantined was like a living hell. She was discharged, but not totally freed; she was smiling but not totally happy. Sometimes, she felt like dying was the right thing that should have happened to her. She felt like being among the dead who did not discriminate against her was better than being amongst the living who stoned her with words. The worst things were said about those who survived and the best things were forgotten about the heroes and heroines who laid down their lives.

With fear of being stigmatized, Patience spent most of her days indoors. Flashes of the horrible scenes of the epidemic still haunted her. Sometimes while sitting, her body jittered at flashes of terror that crossed her mind.

Months later, Patience moved back to live with her aunty in Shara Community and continued life. Though she found it difficult to be reintegrated into her community, she finally overcame the bruises of the epidemic and the crucifixion of being a victim of Ebola. Like a moving train, she kept moving on with her life. She had not forgiven the year 2014 nor had she forgotten the memories of its pains.

Siatta, Jackson, Gray and Grace were taken at the ETU in Gbarnga and were all tested negative. As for Famatta, Hellen and Patience, they were tested positive. Ma. Malah and Ma. Korto were preventive and did not show signs of the virus nor fall sick. Hellen who was pregnant did not survive along with her unborn child.

At last, after the dust settled, only Famatta and Patience who were Ebola-positive survived the storm that rigidly blew the leaves of their family tree, including Daniel.

As for the driver who drove Patience's family to town and interacted with the Stewarts, his whereabouts remain unknown. Maybe his ashes may have returned to ashes or he too survived and concealed the horrible stories of the epidemic beneath the melanin of his skin.

Gradually, cases of Ebola in Liberia were reducing and more people were being treated and discharged. May 2015 was when Liberia was first declared Ebola-free. Subsequently, few cases were found and treated, and the country was again declared Ebola-free in mid-September 2015. Even though few more cases were discovered in November 2015 and treated, long observation was carried out. On January 14, 2016, Liberia was again declared Ebola-free; however, few cases were detected in March and April of 2016, and Liberia made its final declaration on June 1, 2016, a free land of liberty by God's command.

Since the land of West Africa was finally declared Ebola-free, minds swore never to divorce the memories of the year 2014; for the matrimony that unified them filled their cups with sorrows and made them tossed against a glass of calamity.

As the orchestra of mourning played, those who danced could no longer dance so they stood in awe; those who sang could no longer sing, so they hummed; and those who feasted on bowls of grief were filled so much that they threw out instead.

For Patience, August is Unforgotten – the same month she was born, the same month she lost the one to whom she was born. It is certain for sure; sometime again, the world will wrap herself in another blanket of an epidemic and fall asleep; deep into solitude's land. Sometime again, the sun will rise and warm the coating of her wrinkled skin, trading its radiance for her pain.

Unforgotten as it came, unforgotten it may come again. But until then, let this be inscribed in stones that when '*August*' comes again, the disbelief of the ones breathing will not cause them to dance with death on the stage of life.

POEM

Unforgotten August

For our remains, there are no graves

Our flesh and bones were set ablaze.

The thick-skinned wears deep scars

Seen only by the pure in hearts.

In fear and tears, we clothed

And wrapped beneath blankets of snow.

Notes of mourning were all that played

As we danced to tormenting nights and days.

Like a tidal wave, August raged,

Unforgotten, our smiles it caged.

We tossed our pains against LIFE

Yet, we stooped to the trumpets of DEATH

We've travelled far to Heaven's land

Where clouds and stars are felt with hands;
A land from whence no traveler returns
And flesh and bone in summer burns.

For us, it's midnight,

too dark to learn,

no wage to earn,

but to the living, may that August never return.

PUZZLE

This puzzle contains 77 words that were used in this book. Locate the given words below running in a horizontal, vertical, diagonal, backward, forward and upward direction.

```
L S P V I U W I L D F I R E C C D P P S E Y N E H
K L A H R N Y I S W J G N F P E I V E S O H A P E
W I I S Q E H V R Z I Z H L T L F C A S O L H O R
K C B B N A B N X F P Q T S L A A E U P P P P N B
I E N O W R B L A P P A E S M P S R S D B R R Y A
E B O L A T U U X P E F B I S I F C E M E T O M L
G K L H D H R D E S N N L U D C O A A N E Z L C I
S R R A E C I K D I X Y L K Q T I L M H U Y O S S
G P A I N A A Y N O M E R E C X A O A N Q F R O T
N L G D E F L F I Y Q E H H A R L K W E E E L P O
I P N E E N H T D C M J I B I G R A M R V A I B P
N A I N W N E U H A T A K A K L A U T I R T B I N
R T K I O S D I I C Y K P A C L H B U S Z P E H E
U I C T U E S N G E A M E O N I E Q J U C S R J W
O E A N N N S X A H E R V O T S A A A A L A I O R
M N H A D O U R U P B U E S U R I V R W M G A U E
U C W R E Z N R J T A O R U D R A E Y N Q B H R D
K E D A D E K K U J Z N R B X E G O S P E L O N E
E O U U D T C O J D R I I H E J L N U R J O D E M
G R P Q S I S O L A T E D C O D U D I U A U A Y P
P N A U S E A T I N G J Z Y L O U W N N M C X G T
A L G R E C K O N E D L V A W E D C P I A P S Z I
Z U E C N E D N E P E D N I R O D O C V K L I Y O
A L A C I G O L O H C Y S P S Y M P T O M S E Z N
T R E A T M E N T G G M R O T S R E D N U H T M N
```

Words Bank

August	Herbalist	Melanin
Awe	Hopscotch	Mourning
Bed	Ill	Mud
Burial	Independence	Nauseating
Capsule	Index	Neighborhood
Ceremony	Infested	New
Corpse	Isolated	Nooks
Dawn	Jambo	Odor
Disease	Journey	Oozed
Ebola	Joy	Orphan
End	Kakata	Outbreak
Eponym	Kindled	Pain
Family	Kola	Panic
Fed	Kru	Patience
Funeral	Lappa	Pills
Gasp	Learn	Psychological
God	Liberia	Quarantined
Gospel	Malaria	Quivers
Healthcare	Margibi	Reckoned

Redemption

Remains

Ritual

Scars

Sick

Siren

Symptoms

Thunderstorm

Top

Treatment

Unearth

Vai

Virus

Whacking

Wildfire

Wounded

Year

Yearned

Zip

Zones

www.ingramcontent.com/pod-product-compliance
Lightning Source LLC
Chambersburg PA
CBHW070543160726
48003CB00005B/1858